M.I.A.

By Lynn Peppas

D1511744

Crabtree Publishing Company
www.crabtreebooks.com

Crabtree Publishing Company
www.crabtreebooks.com

Author: Lynn Peppas
Publishing plan research and development:
  Sean Charlebois, Reagan Miller
  Crabtree Publishing Company
Project coordinator: Kathy Middleton
Photo research: Crystal Sikkens
Editors: Molly Aloian, Kathy Middleton
Proofreader and Indexer: Wendy Scavuzzo
Designer: Ken Wright
Production coordinator and
  Prepress technician: Ken Wright

Photographs:
Associated Press: pages 1, 6, 8, 9, 26
BigStockPhoto: page 11
Dreamstime.com: page 5 (bottom)
Getty Images: Steven Henry/Stringer:
  pages 10, 22; Chris McKay/WireImage:
  page 18 (left); Kevin Winter: page 24; Jeffrey
  Ofberg/WireImage: page 27; Andy Sheppard/
  Redferns: page 28
Keystone Press: © Jason Moore/ Zumapress.com
  page 4; Aviv Small/Zumapress.com: page 21;
  John Barrett/Zumapress.com: page 25
Retna Pictures: © Gregory Warran/
  www.rmusic.co.uk: cover; © George Chin/
  www.rmusic.co.uk: page 5 (top); Chris Clunn
  pages 12 (bottom), 13; Mike Schreiber: page 1
  Robin/Retnauk: page 16; Katinka Herbert:
  page 19; Peter Everard Smith: page 20
Jack Schulze/Phil Baines © 1997, 2002: page 15
Shutterstock: page 7, 12 (top), 18 (right)
Wikipedia: DJFLEX-mk2: page 17

Every effort has been made to trace copyright holders and to obtain their permission for use of copyright material. The authors and publishers would be pleased to rectify any error or omission in future editions. All the Internet addresses given in this book were correct at the time of going to press. The author and publishers regret any inconvenience caused if addresses have changed or sites have ceased to exist, but can accept no responsibility for any such changes.

Library and Archives Canada Cataloguing in Publication

Peppas, Lynn
    M.I.A. / by Lynn Peppas.

(Superstars!)
Includes index.
Issued also in an electronic format.
ISBN 978-0-7787-7249-1 (bound).--ISBN 978-0-7787-7258-3 (pbk.)

    1. M.I.A (Musician)--Juvenile literature. 2. Singers--Biography--Juvenile literature. I. Title. II. Series: Superstars! (St. Catharines, Ont.)

ML3930.M618P42 2011   j782.42164092   C2010-904672-2

Library of Congress Cataloging-in-Publication Data

Peppas, Lynn.
    M.I.A. / by Lynn Peppas.
        p. cm. -- (Superstars!)
    Includes index.
    ISBN 978-0-7787-7258-3 (pbk. : alk. paper) -- ISBN 978-0-7787-724
(reinforced library binding : alk. paper) -- ISBN 978-1-4271-9554-8
(electronic (pdf)
    1. M.I.A (Musician)--Juvenile literature. 2. Singers--Biography--
Juvenile literature. I. Title. II. Series.

ML3930.M06P46 2011
782.42164092--dc22
[B]
                                                              2010027906

Crabtree Publishing Company
www.crabtreebooks.com   1-800-387-7650

Printed in the USA/102010/SP20100915

Published in Canada
Crabtree Publishing
616 Welland Ave.
St. Catharines, ON
L2M 5V6

Published in the United States
Crabtree Publishing
PMB 59051
350 Fifth Avenue, 59th Floor
New York, New York 10118

Published in the United Kingdom
Crabtree Publishing
Maritime House
Basin Road North, Hove
BN41 1WR

Published in Austral
Crabtree Publishing
386 Mt. Alexander Rd.
Ascot Vale (Melbourne)
VIC 3032

CONTENTS

Words that are defined in the glossary are in **bold** type the first time they appear in the text.

Meet M.I.A. ★ ★

Four gunshots go off, "boom, boom, boom, boom," and a cash register rings "cha-ching." In most songs, people play instruments, such as guitars or drums, and create rhythms and melodies. But M.I.A.'s international hit song "Paper Planes" takes a different path. The female rapper is a true artist who creates cutting-edge music. In her original music, she uses sounds as symbols, along with different beats and rhythms from around the world.

"Paper Planes" Takes Flight

The singer/songwriter's career really took flight from popular to superstar musician with the release of "Paper Planes." The song became familiar to many people because it was on the **soundtracks** to the movies *Pineapple Express* and *Slumdog Millionaire*.

Who Is M.I.A.?

M.I.A. is the stage name for musician and artist Mathangi Arulpragasam. She goes by the name "Maya." M.I.A. is an **acronym** for "missing in action." This phrase is used to describe people who are unaccounted for after a military mission or battle. To Maya, the phrase also stands for "missing in Acton." Acton is an area in London, England, where Maya once lived.

On the Move

Maya was born in England. The family moved to Sri Lanka, the country where her parents were born, when Maya was a baby. She spent most of her younger years in Sri Lanka during a time when the country was torn by **civil war**. Maya, her mother, and her two siblings escaped back to England as **refugees** when she was almost ten. Her experiences of living in a time of war and becoming a refugee have greatly **influenced** her art and music.

She Said It

"I can sing about songs with gunshots in the background because I'd heard them. It's almost like my music has been a way to smoke out the hatred that's been bubbling underneath what's going on in Sri Lanka. If there's 300,000 people who are trapped and they're dying, it should be talked about. It should be brought to the table..."
—Video interview for *www.time.com*, April 2009

Where Is Sri Lanka?

Sri Lanka is a country in Asia, just off the southern tip of India. More than 21 million people live in Sri Lanka. The majority of the people are Sinhalese. They speak the language called Sinhala. Most of the other people in Sri Lanka are Tamil, and they speak the Tamil language. Maya and her family are Tamil.

INDIA

BANGLADESH

Calcutta

Chennai

SRI LANKA

An Artist in More Ways Than One

When Maya began her career, she wasn't looking to make her fame and fortune in the music industry. She wanted to be an artist and graphic designer. A graphic designer is a person who creates advertisements and pamphlets using images and words put together in an attention-grabbing way.

She Said It

"It wasn't really about getting fame and success and becoming a celebrity and selling records. It was more about bringing together an opinion or a point of view of 'the other' that doesn't usually get heard in the **mainstream**."
—Interview with Tavis Smiley, January 2009

Accidental Artist

Maya became a musician almost by accident. She started working as a **visual** artist and was hired by the members of a rock band to design an album cover. She began hanging around other musicians, which led her to experiment with making her own music. She discovered that she loved creating music—and that people loved listening to what she created. The director Spike Jonze met Maya in 2005 at the beginning of her music career. "She insisted she wasn't a musician," he said. "To this day, she doesn't consider herself a musician."

Club Culture Music

M.I.A.'s catchy rhythms and beats are perfect to dance to and, in the beginning of Maya's music career, her songs were played by **DJ**'s in dance clubs throughout Britain. Today, her songs are played throughout the world. M.I.A.'s songs are described as a kind of world music that combines elements of different **genres**, including hip hop, rap, reggae, electronica, and dancehall.

Fans around the world get up and dance to M.I.A.'s songs.

Political Activist

M.I.A. doesn't just entertain people with her music. She uses music to try to make people aware of different political situations in the world. She is a political activist—a person who tries to tell others about a political situation and change their opinions about it. Common themes in her music are **social injustice**, war, and the position in society of refugees, whom she often calls "the other."

A Different Type of Childhoo

Mathangi Arulpragasam was born in London, England. Although there is some question as to whether she was born in 1975 or 1977, M.I.A. tells fans she was born on July 17, 1977. When she was six months old, her family moved to her parents' native country, Sri Lanka. Maya lived with her mother and older sister, Kali, on her grandparents' farm, which had no electricity or running water. Maya's brother, Sugu, was born after they moved to Sri Lanka.

TRY TO IMAGINE

While growing up, Maya experienced a lifestyle that most kids could never even imagine. During the war in Sri Lanka, Maya saw people taken by force from her village. Her school and even her own house were burned down.

Civil War

At the time Maya's family returned, Sri Lanka was torn by war. For about 150 years, the country had been a **colony** of Britain. In 1948, it gained its **independence**, and the Sinhalese majority of people formed the government. They began taking **citizenship** away from the Tamil people. They also made Sinhala the country's only official language.

A commander gives instructions to fellow Tamil Tigers.

Protesting New Laws

Some of the Tamil people protested against the new laws. In 1976, some Tamils organized a military group called the Liberation Tigers of Tamil Eelam, also known as the Tamil Tigers. The Tamil Tigers wanted to separate from Sri Lanka and form their own country. In 1983, civil war broke out between the Tamil Tigers and the Sri Lankan army. Riots broke out and angry mobs of Sinhalese people destroyed Tamil-owned homes and businesses and killed many Tamil people, including those who did not belong to the Tamil Tigers.

Tamil citizens visit a cemetery for Tamil Tigers.

A Child of War

The war lasted many years. It ended in May 2009 when the last of the Tamil Tigers were defeated. In the army's effort to win, many innocent people were killed. During the war, more than 80,000 people were officially listed as killed. Some estimate that many more died. Many of the men, women, and children killed were innocent citizens.

Meet the Parents

Maya's father Arul Pragasam joined the Tamil fight for independence when his family returned to Sri Lanka. Maya and her siblings did not see their father very much growing up. He had to hide from the Sri Lankan army. He went by the name "Arular" and joined a Tamil military group of students. Maya named her first full-length album *Arular* after her father. Her mother Kala was the complete opposite of her father. Kala focused on raising Maya and her brother and sister. Maya's second album *Kala* was named after her mother.

She Said It

"*[My Dad] was really into ideas and stuff like that, and saving the planet, and you know, like revolution…And my mum was the opposite…She put food on the table because she just wanted to save three people, and I thought that's just as important…*"
—Interview on Canadian current affairs show *The Hour*, October 2007

M.I.A. poses with her second album *Kala*.

She Said It

"When we tried to leave Sri Lanka with my mom, the buses we were on would be stopped in the middle of nowhere and people would be taken off and killed. It teaches you how bad human beings can be."
—Interview with Joshua Ostroff in *Eye Weekly*, January 27, 2005

Move to India

It became too dangerous for Maya, her mother, and siblings to live in Sri Lanka during the civil war. Maya's father sent them tickets to move to Madras, now called Chennai, in India. Once there, they had very little money, and Maya's sister became sick with typhoid fever. They moved back to Sri Lanka and tried to escape to another country.

Music: M.I.A.'s Universal Language

When Maya was ten years old, she moved to London with her mother and siblings. Her father remained in Sri Lanka. Maya could barely speak any English. She had to learn English after they arrived in England. What Maya did understand was music.

Music is often called a "universal language" because people everywhere can usually understand the emotion behind the words and music, even if they can't understand the **lyrics**.

LISTEN AND LEARN

Maya was always interested in music, even in Sri Lanka. Most of the music she heard there was pop. Her move to London opened her ears to new sounds in music, such as rap and hip hop. She says that she learned English by listening to rap and hip hop artists like Eric B. & Rakim and Public Enemy.

Hip hop group Public Enemy

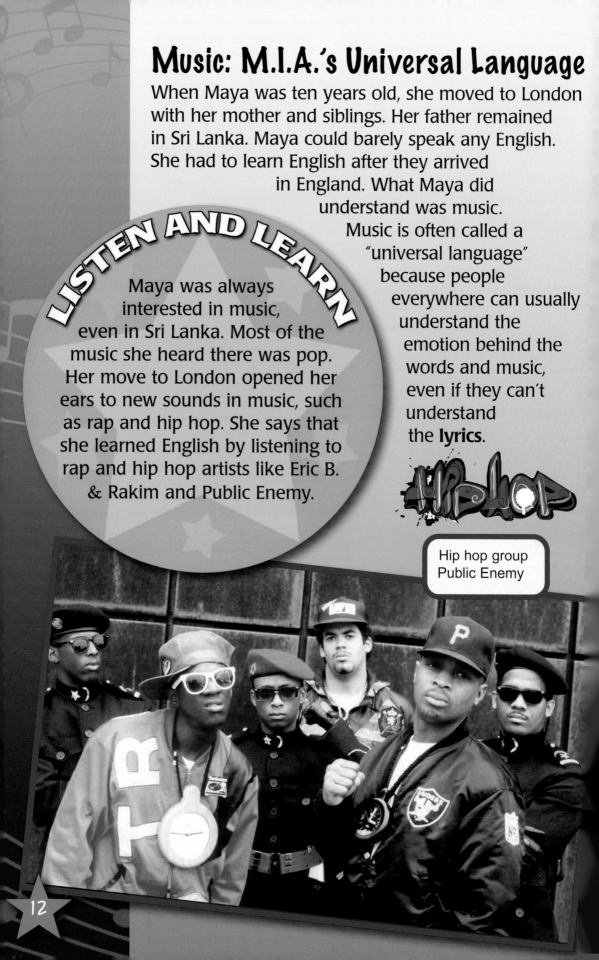

A New Home in London

Maya's mother settled with her children in a council estate in Mitcham, a part of London. Council estates are public housing units in Britain. These homes are rented at low rates to people who cannot afford to pay high rents. Maya remembered it as a rough time in her life, when people were often **prejudiced** against her. Also, people living near her would often steal things like radios and running shoes. Even so, Maya said,

> *"It wasn't as bad as where we came from, where you were running for your lives."*
> —Interview with Chris Mugan in *The Independent*, October 2004

Eric B. & Rakim

School Days

Maya was a good student when she went to school in India, but school was difficult for her in England since she did not speak English well. She also has a learning disorder that makes reading and writing difficult. She wound up spending a great deal of time drawing and doing other types of art.

M.I.A

She Said It

"Even when I was very young, people would get me to draw for them," she remembered, *"but when I came to England, it was the only thing I could do. Because I couldn't speak English very well…teachers would let me go off and paint drama sets instead."*
—Interview with Chris Mugan in *The Independent*, October 2004

Making It Through

During the first ten years of Maya's life, she grew up around war and poverty. She and her family escaped to London where she was treated differently because she was a refugee. She concentrated on the things that she was good at and loved: music and art. The arts are what got her through her teen years growing up in London.

Central Saint Martins College of Art and Design

Maya knew she was good at the arts, such as drawing and making videos. She pursued her talent in art after high school. She attended the Central Saint Martins College of Art and Design in London, where she studied fine art, film, and video.

Developing a Career

Justine Frischmann, lead singer from the British alternative rock band, Elastica, was impressed with Maya's talents and hired her to do the artwork for the band's album *The Menace* which was released in 2000. After this opportunity, Maya—who had also studied video in college—videotaped the band on their U.S. tour. The band also had her direct a music video for one of the songs on the album.

Elastica seen here in 2000.

The Roland MC-505

Maya videotaped Elastica's U.S. tour in 2003. While on tour, she met a Canadian musician named Peaches who owned a Roland MC-505 sequencing drum machine. The machine can record **samples** of sounds and beats. It also contains different rhythms and sounds that can be layered into a song. When she returned to London, Maya bought her own Roland MC-505 and started experimenting, trying to create her own music. She wrote some of her first songs, such as "M.I.A." and "Galang," with Justine Frischmann using the Roland MC-505.

Roland MC-505

Returning to Sri Lanka

After she graduated from art school in 2001, Maya returned to Sri Lanka for a visit. She wanted to film a **documentary** about what had happened to her cousin, whom she had grown up with. He had become a Tamil Tiger, or freedom fighter for the Tamil cause. Maya had heard he had recently died. According to an interview with Maya in *Rolling Stone* magazine, Maya's mother knew it was too dangerous for Maya to film what was happening in Sri Lanka. She locked Maya in a bedroom in the home they were staying at and wouldn't let her out.

The experience of being back in Sri Lanka awakened Maya's sense of responsibility. She knew she had to try to bring about some sort of awareness of the Tamil people caught in the war-torn country—and try to change their situation.

She Said It

"[My cousin and I] were partners…when we were kids, soul mates. At 10, I left. He stayed and joined the Tigers. He died the same week I graduated with a fine-arts degree…It was just amazing to me that someone my age, who had the same start I did, who was better in school than I was…ended up dead. And I didn't."
–Interview in *Rolling Stone* magazine, December 2005

Exhibiting Her Art

In 2001, Maya's first public art exhibition was held at the Euphoria Shop in London. She showed a series of paintings done in a **graffiti** style. Her artwork featured Tamil **revolutionary** images mixed with images of life in London. The exhibition was a great success, and the show was nominated for the Alternative Turner Prize—a British visual art award.

In 2002, the British publisher Pocko published Maya's artwork in a book called *M.I.A.: No. 10*. In the book, there are **stenciled** images of colorful tigers, soldiers, guns, and a woman's face shown with English phrases such as "Deaf Ears, Death Nears." Some of the words are written in Tamil. Maya's art style is called graffiti or stencil art. Stencils are cut-out letters and images that are repeated in an artwork. Sometimes the stencils are spray-painted. It makes it look as though it were created on the street as graffiti.

An Early Following

Musicians Steve Mackey and Ross Orton helped Maya rework a demonstration version of "Galang" into the version it is today, and Showbiz Records released the single in 2003, under the name M.I.A. Disc jockeys at dance clubs in Britain started playing her music. Maya also released "Galang" on the Internet along with other songs such as "Sunshowers." That gained her an international, **underground** following. The songs also attracted interest from major record **labels**, such as XL Recordings. The label signed Maya to record her **debut** album. XL also re-released "Galang" for a wider audience.

Arular

Maya's first album *Arular* was supposed to be released in 2004, but wasn't released until 2005. It was delayed because she had to get permission to use samples of sounds she'd added to her songs. In her songs on *Arular*, for example, she used sounds made by toys she had bought in India.

Working Together

M.I.A.'s fans were eager for the album to come out. She met and worked with an American musician named DJ Diplo. They used some of M.I.A.'s songs to produce the album, *Piracy Funds Terrorism, Volume 1*, in the United States in 2004. Together they mixed M.I.A.'s songs with parts of other artists' music to make a new song. The album was never officially released. Diplo and M.I.A. made a few thousand copies and M.I.A.'s record label XL Recordings distributed them to **promote** M.I.A. Diplo also sold some CDs when he played in clubs and at shows.

M.I.A. promoting her *Arular* album

20

Rave Reviews!

Arular was a big success. The album got rave reviews from music magazines and audiences all over the world. To promote the album, Maya went on an international tour that included performances in North America, South America, Europe, and Asia. She also opened a number of dates during Gwen Stefani's late 2005 tour. "Arular *hit me by surprise,*" Maya said. "*Everything happened so fast. The fact that America responded to what I was making made me feel like I do have faith in the human race...*"
—Interview on *MTV ADD Bio,* September 2007

M.I.A. performs in New York City on her *Arular* tour.

The Journey of an Artist

M.I.A. has continued to develop as an artist in many different areas. In doing so, she has shown that even a person from humble beginnings can accomplish a great deal. As she said in 2009,

"I think the journey in the beginning as an artist for me was to show that you can make the jump from being a refugee to being whoever you want to be."
—Interview for the "100 Top Influential People of 2009" in *Time 100*

M.I.A. promotes her new album *Kala* at a bookstore in New York.

Kala

Arular introduced M.I.A.'s music to many new listeners, but it was her second album *Kala* that took her from being a popular recording artist and musician to being a superstar. *Kala* was released in August 2007 by Interscope Records. Maya was supposed to do most of the recording and production of the album in the United States, but her **visa** ran out and she had to return to Britain. She wound up doing much of the recording and production of the album in different locations around the world, such as Trinidad, India, and Liberia.

Shortly after *Kala* came out, M.I.A. said everything [on the album]

> "...is built out of wherever I've gone...I took all of the songs to India, then I took all of the songs to Trinidad, then I took all of the songs to Jamaica. Every song has a layer of some other country on it."

—Interview with Alex Wagner in *The Fader* magazine, August 2007

Sending a Message

The chorus of "Paper Planes" features lyrics and different sounds. The words of the chorus are: "All I wanna do is [sounds of a gun shooting and reloading and a cash register ringing] and take your money." Maya says she wrote the song because she felt that many people think that **immigrants** and refugees don't contribute to the societies they live in. Instead, these people think immigrants and refugees only take from society. She may not say these exact words in the song, but the message comes through in her sound effects. She also created the song as a piece of art that is supposed to make listeners think of what it means to them personally. In this way, the meaning of the song's lyrics and sounds are open to **interpretation**, just like a painting or drawing.

"PAPER PLANES"

Even though *Kala* was released in 2007, the album's hit single "Paper Planes," which she wrote with DJ Diplo, did not gain its enormous popularity until a year later. In 2008, it was used in a TV **trailer** for the movie *Pineapple Express*.

Retirement Rumors

In June 2008, M.I.A. was performing at the Bonnaroo Music Festival in Manchester, Tennessee. She announced to her fans during the concert that it was her "last show ever." Shortly after this, she canceled her European tour. It seemed like the retirement rumor was really true. Her "retirement" didn't last very long, though. By October 2008, she was onstage again, performing in Brooklyn, New York. She also got an offer from *Slumdog Millionaire* movie director Danny Boyle that she just couldn't resist.

Slumdog Millionaire Success

Danny Boyle was a fan of M.I.A.'s music, and he knew he wanted the song "Paper Planes" in the score to his movie. He asked M.I.A. if he could use

M.I.A. and A.R. Rahman perform the songs "Jai Ho" and "O... Saya" from the movie *Slumdog Millionaire*.

her song. She watched the movie and agreed. M.I.A. was also a big fan of A.R. Rahman, who wrote the award-winning soundtrack for *Slumdog Millionaire*. Rahman and M.I.A. worked together to write another song that was included on the soundtrack, as well. It was called "O... Saya." *Slumdog Millionaire* was a very successful movie, and it won the Academy Award for best picture of 2008.

The popularity of the movie meant that even more people heard M.I.A.'s music. The song that she wrote with A.R. Rahman, was nominated for an Academy Award for best original song in 2008.

Benjamin Bronfman

Maya's fiancé is Benjamin Bronfman. He is the son of billionaire Edgar Bronfman, Jr., the head of Warner Music Group. Benjamin Bronfman sometimes goes by the name Ben Brewer. In 2000, Benjamin and two other musicians formed the post-punk reggae band The Exit, with Benjamin playing lead guitar. In 2006, the band broke up. Today, Benjamin is one of the founders of the record label Green Owl Records, which is dedicated to helping the environment. The record company produces records for musicians who are concerned with the environment. Green Owl Records helps the environment by donating all the profits from certain albums to organizations such as Energy Action Coalition. They also produce CD jackets made from recycled paper.

M.I.A. and Ben Brewer at *Time's* 100 Most Influential People in the World gala.

Grammy Baby

When M.I.A. came out of retirement in late 2008, it was clear that she was expecting a baby. The baby was due on February 8, 2009, but Maya didn't take it easy that day. Instead, she was performing at the Grammy Awards. M.I.A. took the stage with famous rappers like Jay-Z, Kanye West, T.I., and Lil Wayne to perform the song she helped write, called "Swagga Like Us." M.I.A. had been nominated for two Grammy Awards, for Best Rap Song for "Swagga Like Us" and Record of the Year for "Paper Planes." She didn't win, but she put on a great show.

M.I.A. and Kanye West perform at the 2009 Grammy Awards.

Other Creative Outlets

M.I.A. is known for her colorful fashion sense. Designer Marc Jacobs cashed in on Maya's fashionable coolness in 2008, when he hired her to DJ at a party following one of his fashion shows. He also had M.I.A. model for his Spring/Summer 2008 collection ad campaign. Because she is so important to the current music scene—as well as so striking—M.I.A. has been featured on the covers of different music magazines. *Time* magazine listed her as one of the top 100 influential people who most affected the world in 2009.

Her Own Label

In the fall of 2008, M.I.A. started producing other musicians' music under her own record label N.E.E.T. The name stands for "Not engaged in Employment, Education, or Training" and is a term used by the British government to describe young people who are not participating in society. The record label's first release was the *Slumdog Millionaire* soundtrack. The album hit the number one spot on the U.S. Billboard Top Electronic Album chart in 2009.

M.I.A. and her son Ikhyd arrive at the *Late Night Show with David Letterman* studio on July 13, 2010.

And the Award Goes To...

M.I.A. has been nominated for many awards, including two Grammy Awards and an Academy Award. The Academy Award nomination was for best song, for *Slumdog Millionaire*'s "O... Saya." In 2009, she won a BET Award for Best Female Hip Hop Artist, a Brit Award for British Female Solo Artist, and two ASCAP Awards for songs she co-wrote—"Paper Planes" and "Swagga Like Us."

The Future

In January 2010, M.I.A. released a new song and video called "Space Odyssey" on her Twitter site. The video shows her moving to the beat, lit up only by green lights. The music is different from anything she has done before. M.I.A.'s third album, named using a series of slashes that spell out *MAYA*, was released in July 2010. She worked on the album with musician and producer Blaqstarr and has said the new release has "different sounding beats" and more singing and rapping than *Kala*. A lot of the rhythms on *MAYA* are inspired by dance club beats. Yet, like her other albums, M.I.A.'s politics are a central theme of many of the songs' lyrics. The video for the single "Born Free" was banned from YouTube for showing violent imagery. M.I.A. toured through the summer of 2010 to promote the new album.

A World of Influence

What does the future hold for M.I.A.? That's hard to say. As she said in late 2009, "Every time I make plans, totally the opposite happens." She continues to work with other musicians, such as Christina Aguilera, on their music. She also works on her own music with other musicians, such as Diplo and Blaqstarr. But it was never her plan to only make music for a living, and she has often felt uncomfortable being described as a musician. In December 2009, M.I.A. told *Rolling Stone* magazine that "(My) next album is not me saying, 'Hi, I'm a musician now,' but 'Am I a musician?'" One thing is clear, though: M.I.A. is influenced by what is going on around her and continues to influence the world of music and art. She proves that one small voice can make a big difference in the world.

Timeline

1977: Mathangi "Maya" Arulpragasam is born in Britain on July 17.

1983: Maya, her mother, sister, and brother move from Sri Lanka to India, then back to Sri Lanka.

1987: Maya's family moves to London as refugees.

2000: M.I.A. designs the cover for Elastica's album *The Menace*. She also videotapes their U.S. tour and produces a video of one of their songs.

2001: M.I.A. graduates from Central Saint Martin's College of Art and Design. She takes a trip to Sri Lanka, then holds her first art exhibit in London.

2002: Pocko Editions publishes a 96-page art book of M.I.A.'s visual art called *M.I.A.: No. 10*.

2003: Showbiz Records releases M.I.A.'s first single "Galang."

2004: M.I.A. signs with XL Recordings and records her debut album *Arular*. The singles "Galang" and "Sunshowers" are re-released.

2004: M.I.A. works with American DJ Diplo on a demo CD *Piracy Funds Terrorism, Volume 1*.

2005: *Arular* is released in March.

2005: M.I.A. tours in November as an opening act on Gwen Stefani's Harajuku Lovers Tour.

2007: M.I.A.'s second album *Kala* is released by Interscope Records in August.

2008: M.I.A. and Benjamin Bronfman get engaged.

2008: M.I.A. announces her retirement in June.

2008: "Paper Planes" is used in the trailer for the movie *Pineapple Express*.

2008: M.I.A. starts N.E.E.T. Recordings. Its first release is the soundtrack for *Slumdog Millionaire*.

2009: M.I.A. is nominated for two Grammy awards.

2009: M.I.A. gives birth to son Ikhyd Edgar Arular Bronfman on February 11.

2010: M.I.A. releases her third album *MAYA* in July.

29

Glossary

acronym A word that is created by taking the first letters of the words in a phrase

citizenship The rights and freedoms that are given to the members of a country or state

civil war A military conflict between two groups of people living in the same country

colony A place that has been settled and is govern or controlled by people from another country

debut Something that is performed for the first tim

DJ An acronym for "disc jockey," a person who selects and plays records on the radio or at a dance or a dance club

documentary A movie or television program abou real-life situations

genre A classification or type of music, art, or writing that shows a particular style

graffiti Pictures or words that are drawn on walls or other surfaces

immigrants People who move to another country to live

independence The state of not being controlled by others

influenced Affected or shaped someone's life or work in an important way

interpretation An understanding about what something means

labels Companies that make and sell recorded music

lyrics The words to a song

mainstream What the majority of people think or do

prejudiced Having an unfair opinion about someone based on his or her culture and nationalit

promote To share information about a product

refugees People who flee to another country to escape danger or difficulty in their native country

evolutionary Supporting a political or social change
n a country's government

ample In music, a small portion of a song

ocial injustice An unfairness in society

oundtracks Albums of the music featured in a
novie or television show

tenciled Cut a pattern or letter in a thin sheet of
netal, cardboard, or plastic, and produced the
attern on a surface beneath it by applying paint
r ink to the cut-out areas

railer An advertisement for a film or television
rogram that consists of small bits of the film

nderground People who think and act in
riginal ways and do not follow mainstream
deas and actions

isa An official document that allows a person
o enter a foreign country

isual Having to do with seeing

ind Out More

Websites

www.myspace.com/mia
www.miauk.com
http://twitter.com/_M_I_A_
www.neetrecordings.com/

Books

Arulpragasam, Maya, with Inigo Asis and Nicola
  Schwartz (Eds.) *M.I.A.: No. 10. London, UK:* Pocko
  Editions, 2002.

Index

About the Author

Lynn Peppas is a writer of children's nonfiction books. She has always been a bookworm and grew up reading all the books she could. She feels fortunate to have been able to combine her love of reading and her love of kids into a career. Her work in children's publishing is a dream-job come true.